3/2

MW00570410

GOD
ON HIS
HAUNCHES

GOD
ON HIS
HAUNCHES

DIANE L.
TUCKER

NIGHTWOOD
EDITIONS

Nightwood Editions
R.R.2 • S.26 • C. 3
Gibsons • BC V0N 1V0 • Canada

Cover art and design by Kim LaFave.
Author photograph by Jim Tucker.
Page design & layout by David Lee Communications.

Published with the assistance of the Canada Council and the
Government of British Columbia, Cultural Services Branch.
Printed and bound in Canada.

Canadian Cataloguing in Publication Data

Tucker, Diane L. (Diane Lynne), 1965–
God on his haunches

Poems.
ISBN 0-88971-163-1

I. Title.
PS8589.U28G62 1996   C811'.54   C96-910570-3
PR9199.3.T74G62 1996

For Elizabeth Hope, who
made this poetry stuff
possible again.

Acknowledgments

I would like to thank first of all my parents, who raised me to do what I love and do it as well as I can. Next I must thank certain teachers: Susan, John, Jerry and especially Alban and George. These teachers helped me surprise myself, and gave me confidence, a wanton love of metaphor and a lust for the power of *the right word*.

I must also give heartfelt thanks to all my friends in the Burnaby Writers' Society, a group that has quietly and faithfully nurtured dozens of fine writers all over the place long before I had anything whatever to do with it.

Many thanks to the journals that published many of the poems that appear herein: *Grail: an ecumenical journal, Green's Magazine, Manna, The Rolling Coulter, Aerings, Deep South, Studio: a journal of christians writing, The Carleton Arts Review, The New Quarterly, Canadian Literature*.

Finally, thanks, of course, to the helpful people at Nightwood Editions, particularly Marisa Alps and John Pass. Thank you for encouraging me to find out what I truly mean and really really say it. Now I feel confirmed, and can let the words dig deeper.

Diane L. Tucker

Contents

for my biological father

you are a breath stirring at the edge of the playground
at the very very top of the monkey bars
mystery breathes on my bare shoulders
whispers between my spread-eagled arms:
you could be anyone in the whole wide world

you are in the mist of years a potent shadow
bereft of the dignity of law and birth, haunting me
only genetically, silent atop that double helix
never your grand entrance down that spiral staircase
strangers precede you, slide blithely down the banister
roll out the carpet for one another
rampant in the red game of my life

you up there can you tell me
among all this merriment arisen
since I dropped like a hot coal into my family's eager mouth
why am I still standing here
letting them frolic past me down that path
why am I still standing here
looking for your shadow as if you hadn't disappeared
sensibly left this mistake, this blip
and marched on into the rest of your life

leaving me shrouded in your double helix
like a dead man wrapped in my country's flag

again it is the time

Again it is the time I trace your brow
    forged in thick, warm bone
and pronounce your features timeless
    if not handsome.
I am able to kiss the hinge of your jaw,
    under your ear, just now,
to feel the stubble burn
    my lips as you shiver.
Your face turns to face me.
    Stark strong cheek moves
under the narrow light,
    opens lips to breathe, to speak,
your voice heavy as a crossbow,
    dark as its wood.

The Community Relations of
a Certain Ms. Nevin

I. Ms. Nevin appears:

Ah, that scarlet spill of hair —
   rich soup.
Like pastry, you've layered your statuesque sorrow
   across the creamy shelf of your cheek
   stained into your jaw
   raised in desperate poetry.

   Your collarbone —
   oft kissed —
rises from the silk of you.

You are adorned with fingers,
   the nails filed, golden.
You have such balletic fingers
   to stroke the stem of the wine glass.
   On your lips drops cling,
   golden.

Like the raising of a curtain,
you smile.

II. Ms. Nevin seeks:

Strong-willed lips, all around you now.
You'll find the pair
that will fall against your lips,
against your collarbone —
oft kissed.
The thin, pearlescent bone,
your brave chiming voice
a buoyant sound
a bubble — burst
by strong-willed lips
covering yours —
two pungent wines, mingled.

Lust is so clear. Bodies, not words.
The self's simplest exit.
It is never complex.

Your shoes, with their
heels like lances, drop
from the edge of the bedspread.
You become a sharp
object.

III. Ms. Nevin speaks:

"There's never time for silence.

One day I'll shut off all this sociable noise
about sculpture
stanzas
string quintets.
I'll stand staring at the sea,
steep my stilled brain, finally,
in thought.

But now there's no space for silence,
just for scampi and smoked salmon,
smiles over white wine spritzers
on this vast pale terrace
glassed in
against the reaching sun,
against the sky."

Old Soul

Drunk on kisses
from some bacchanal
where breath is wine,
you blast obliterating laughter.

Yet there are moments
you forget the wit of it all
and stretch
to fill the artist of your pretense
with blood that's more than wine.
Just as you open to pour something ripe,
something living,
your lip curls back like singed hair.
You say something
charming.

Swan in the lap of Leda
you sit:
a whelming wingéd shadow,
a changeling
spent.

your cool car

when we were young dancers it was
step ball change step ball change
back to the coda one more refrain
then you could sit
drink the night
like black gatorade

and your car door opened
my bottom slipped along the cool vinyl
and I was ready for anything:
that open door
that table that beer
that low-tide voice
those bottomless
black pit eyes

but it wasn't you — it was your car
your cool car
it was the wind we made when we went too fast
it was night tangled in my hair like seaweed
it was skin like sand in my clothes
it was air finally cool enough to breathe
it was grass wet as eyes
it wasn't you

Will I wait?

when I have waited
how long have I waited?

in clouds of prayer
crowded against the ceiling

in the shade of your shielded eyes
turned from mine
in crackle yellow air where windpieces cut
where gazes broke, not cleanly
but like crushed biscuits
like bones

> *stretched across the frets*
> *across a string taut*
> *my cries notes from songs*
> *plucked from old nights in arms of warm music*
> *not this music of wire*
> *not this music of stabbing ice*

then in July
wide eyed came I
up to the sound of sweet bells in morning
up from the far away water where you waited
back against the wet grass in the stars watered call
up from trees standing black as unthread needles

up to cold voice of thin and indigo morning
of wind-and-wire island night

will you wait

I love you

here I come

a supine mountain

my body, supine, is a mountain
you, the mountaineer

make your way along the left
leg, turn your ankle next to the
hip socket, stop and gaze across the hill into
the well of the navel
saying nothing, shaking

place one foot on each rib
religiously — step on a crack
break the mountain's back —
rappel around the left breast, hope
for a good foothold on the collarbone
but find it hidden in flesh, scramble
to the ear's entrance
where you stop

consider whether or not to test the cavern
for the quality of its echo
will it keep or cast back your words?

gather a message into your throat
at the last second let out only
breath

this is consistent
you avoid all the mountain's challenges
every cave, crevasse, dark forest
steer clear of the highest peaks

you had intended to rest in the hair
a deep alpine bed
but it's been cropped clean
you stand on the forehead
look back the way you came
congratulate yourself on the ease
of your ascent, settle against
the stubbly hairline, sit
like a birthmark
out of place
but attached

the neighbourhood watches

you're there in your beds and living rooms
in the dark, silent
looking for stars
waiting for the train's whistle
each of you thinks "I am alone,
a flower in the Sahara of sleep"

you pad into your separate kitchens
for a cup of something warm in the hands
memory, like coffee on the tongue
ambushes you with sweet, biting heat

you part curtains with your faces
exhale a mist against various windows
hearing a child's sleepy cry, you turn:
the walls are getting thin

adultery

weigh the warm breast, ripe and heavy in your hand
is it worth the aching gut
to devour this fruit?

wrap fingers round the buttock's hemisphere
to chart this land would you jump
off the world's edge?

rest your pulsing temple on the rising pubic bone
dare you scale this slope and brave
its dizzy airless peak?

hips to hips hammer quickly, strike the nail's head
would you build a house so slapdash
it crashed with one hot breath?

hollows

go   to bed; kiss in passing; close the wet window

run   toenails down your calf in the night; rain calls to darkness "again, again"

turn   my back to you on the mattress; I've made hollows for hips, for ribs

find   my head's dent in the pillow — not too close or i'll feel you breathe

lie   near enough for warmth

lie   far enough away

lie   touching feet

Then you said "Please don't break my heart."

To such a plea what can one say? I am a kindly soul, willing
to ride a hundred miles an hour, your brown arm sliding under my ribs.
For you I ride without a seat belt, willing to be thrown clear at first impact.

At your plea my heart, like a rock, sinks fast, sinks to my guts,
cause I know, I know. . . when you toke up in the lamplight,
when we drive to the pub for one more case.

In the dark you tell me you love me, one hand on the stair, the other aloft,
pulling those three little words out slow, a scarf of light from night's black hat.
Conjuring, even then, your own collapse.

What an insane, what a stupid thing to say. What a completely impossible feat:
Eat the fruit, but don't break its skin. Leave the shell whole, but dig out the meat.

Little Mags

Names on a page, mere black and white
can knock you down like a punch in the throat
(and don't we all want to deliver that blow
pounding out words 'til our knuckles bleed)

I peruse the little mags
alert to all familiar names
when I see a name I know
I buy it, standing them up together

Murray, dark-haired and angular
glasses wide over grave soft mouth
you asked me who are you why can't you so I
unwrapped for you stories, keeping back
the one where the poet finds muse in your face

Janis, open as a shell on the beach
you risked being filled with sea's debris
so the purging surf could scour you clean
man what an icy ass-slapping rush
unearthing yourself as I never dared

Mark, you bastard, you challenged me
to hone the pen razor sharp
engage in wanton truth-telling
soft voice pressing pinning me to it
urgent face bathed in copier light

I was my own most delicate poem
take out a word and I'd fall to pieces
thinking myself too spotless to touch
too alabaster for you to risk embrace

So like Solomon's girl in the Song
searching streets in the dark for her lover
I peruse the little mags
for names I know and wanted to know
friends I let go too soon

For a Woman of Note

I have written before of this golden ghost
this bare-necked enchantress
of two worlds she was

now giving all to song and wine
to the sour haze of hashish
to flying
through the mist of moving silence
outside her window

now infant alone
in her girl's room
on the floor
sipping tea
near the journal of small poetry
and the oboe
on its thin, bent stand

is she still alone
in one room
lips pressed
dragging a brush through her broomstraw hair
in white immobile silence?

if the waves washed you up

what would I do if the waves washed you up
to my feet, your hair afloat
your neck weak and white
upturned palms swollen, fingers full of crushed shells
facial bones bashed in from dark drowning
but the eyes staring, intact

would I drag you out, clutch you to my breast
weep over your salt-washed skin
kiss your tide-torn lips
wrap myself in seaweed bones?

I'd do what I did the last time I saw you:
looking once into your sea-dead eyes
leave you to the waves' insistent mercy

then face down the shore
and walk away
sand grinding penance between my toes

pregnant cat

belly like mine, like a cradle, climbs
leaps to the top of the fence, pads
along it, stomach fur brushing the board
her silence and stealth as strong
as the wind that harries the cedars
which quiver, waving the wind away

she alone pauses
lifts her whiskers, and we wait
on all four points for the sure soon drop
birth's clutch and thrust, the nose to tail rush
that makes a sky full of wind a mere ruffle of buds
a mere stroking hand
at which to flick an ear ·

stretch marks

closest to the pubic bone they're pale,
shadows of the firstborn
silver tracks of my daughter's dwelling

around the navel they're new as my son
deep purple, flame shaped, threading
the waist, pulling the belly beautifully closed,
an overstuffed drawstring bag
worked in fine flesh tapestry

my stomach a mandala, symmetrical
a map of the months
you trace wide with warm fingers

Beth's Dream

Of what can you be dreaming

when in your sleep
the pacifier lolls in the corner of your mouth
and you laugh, laugh
your eyes still closed?

Are you dreaming of that moment
when with shouts, bursting,
they laid you
red-bright and slimy on my breast
and your first cry
knocked tears from your father's tired eyes?

Or are you dreaming
of the first dark era —
curled in a fishless sea
of weightless rolling warmth,
mysterious voices beating out your water dance?

kathy dreams

I keep
dreaming
about you
and it makes
no sense in my dreams your hair
is so brown like the finest horse
you are sleek and dark your eyes
glitter with knowledge we move
slowly silently like we're
underwater your mouth opens in
your big laugh that takes everybody in

suddenly these dreams it's like stirring
the soup pulling everything up
from the bottom of the bowl again
and again exposing it to the cool air
so it won't burn me
so it won't burn me

Beth, four months

her fingertips on my tongue
    are globes of amber salmon roe
    cool smooth
    and salty
    one tap of teeth and they would
    burst energy
    all through me

she curls over my stomach
    her still head
    between my breasts
    I curl fetal round her
    as though she still
    dwelt in me

kathy

your chestnut head
soft in the crook of my arm
smiles in warm coats
and the leaves
crackle

i imagine such a day
every now and then in the Goldberg Variations

when we make external our hearts in one
wordless walk
in autumn
in our frail frost

smiling our eyes
not afraid to hold hands
or hold one another betimes
if cold
to the ankles in dead leaves
of yellow buried

in the very gold sea we are alive
the sky ahead is gold-grey
we walk toward and into
then upon it
unblinking

Poems About You

I write poems about you
about love and babies
skies, theology, but
I don't write about me anymore
I am long gone
my long shadow
slides down the hallway
slides along the wall
when it gets to the window flies away
a ghost of me flown now over the rooftops

I slipped away in 1988
sometime in spring
out the big north-facing window
rushing, gowned in my long shadow
over everybody else's backyard
toward the purple clouds to the west

here where I am
I am not

Summer Evening

Beth in her little bed, screaming
waylaid on the way to sleep
she needs to get there
and I can't take her

so I get out
walk along the creek to the pond
sit on our favourite bench
her ducks are gone
it starts to rain

the creek splitters over the black rocks
raindrops tiptoe on the taut surface of the pond
robins whisper to one another
goodnight john boy goodnight mama

sweet sibilant music, but meaningless
as a pleasant phrase of ancient Greek

how do I know that the robins aren't grieving
wailing over young cat-killed
how do I know the scurrying ants
are en route, are not mad?

Kathleen Denise

mother-by-womb-alone
gazed into my face
pronounced my name
and for a minute there I was
her breathing pink
moment-daughter

then I was gone
a door swung shut
a new-lit candle snuffed

everything I'd ever be
remade
when they changed my name

Kissing Van Gogh

stars over green flame trees
on my Van Gogh coffee mug
Beth must kiss
the orange slice of moon
the church
in the undulating fields
(anchoring them like a tent peg)
the stars
in the riotous sky

round and round the mug we go
kiss the moon
    the church
    the stars
kiss them all again

her face draws back
she watches the steam
pronounces the scene
"hot, hot"

theatre under the stars

can you smell the cold summer sky
the sharp metallic scent of stars
spread like silver jam on the toasted night

surely you smell it, like dew settling late
on the hundreds of chairs when everybody's gone
except us, we're just shadows, uncast by the night

after all that brassy music, dusty artificial light
cheeks and lips painted red, red
all this damp blackness is our comfort, our refuge
this cold, lightless spot where we don't have to say a word

Teddy

squat, plump and grinning,
hangs over the chair
like a mystic
hanging serenely
by his hair.

Baby bats at him,
squeals as he spins and spins.
Under him
she wriggles, transfixed,
hands a blur,
stretching her drooling smile wider
to inhale the motion.

Beth, you baffle philosophy.
The world's weary wisdom
you merrily capsize
with your ravenous eyes,
your fingers chasing
then catching the light.

In these your waving white hands
you grasp the toy sage;
he spins and spins,
addled by your life,
by your
relentless joy.

dance of falling down

her voice and body dance
turn leap and laugh
(not making fun of
look what a geek
laughter but

we are rare and precious
let's deafen the world
with the bells of our love
laughter)

that laughter
— beating out of her round
ribcage
a bird unbarred —
knows everything
about dance:
the choreography of lumps in the throat
executed with open ears
naked from the heart up

her moving mirth knows
that anything
— unexplained exits, dying clowns,
elephants' feet smashing glass,
fucking it up and falling down —
even falling apart
can be a dance

falling in love with a fat man

i will seek you out you brave and gifted fat man i will show you how i
understand your pain your longings your frightened wanderings i will
kiss the very tip of your magnificent pointed nose

you will fly me away to the never never land of love you will be
wearing a green tunic and a hat with a feather you will look like a
giant brussels sprout like a floating lily pad like mary martin with a
sexy goatee

you will appear with peculiar providence at exactly the right time you
will open your arms and sing when you see me you will whisper
lissome syllables you'll finally blow my cover with your
confession-flooded eyes

Deciduous

Alone I grow
among the columns
bearing up sky's temple roof,
alone among the firs.

In the shadow
of their hovering limbs,
verdant in every season,
I alone let loose a sweep of leaves.
The wind shifts autumn's continent,
whisks my empire clean away
piece by crumbling piece.

The firs bear amongst their bodies
my slow dispersing death.

Winter comes.
The firs stand unchanged.
Sap still snakes through every shining needle.
Wind, snow, icy rain,
the towering firs swell green against them all.

I alone,
in my deciduous shadow,
know the stripped relief —
the beauty of the bare brown branch.

in the garden butterflies

in the garden
  butterflies
are flitting
  mating
incandescent
  in the sun

white butterflies
  leafwings greenglowing
dying in the dance
  the flight
the lowing
  over the leaves
of curling sweet pea
  claws of velvet

lighting on leaf
to wrap legs about her

leg of sunlight
  leg of grassblade
wideflung falling
  wing of paleflame

part the leaves and see
  this coupling
  uncloaked

Louise, lost to Alzheimer's

Lately, you've noticed the weeds keep creeping back
into your well-tended gardens, hiding the roses,
choking the carrots and beets.
Being a faithful gardener, and diligent,
you plunge into the undergrowth, determined to pull every one.

We lost you, somehow, in the high grass and dandelions.

In your mind you are young, a long-necked pioneer girl,
holding in your heart visions of your rough green island:
slicing with slender arms the surface of the lake,
sun parting the clouds as you break the surface.

And even on your quest you won't forget
home, son, grandchildren,
watching for you at the edge of the brambles.
But the weeds grow higher.
Every leaf, every vine looks the same as every other.
Only roses haunt your thoughts now.
Somewhere there must be roses.

I picture you breaking through at last,
torn arms smashing the wall of thorns,
eyes narrowing at the sudden light,
widening again to soft grass and bushes,
branches heavy with blooms.
The scent makes you dizzy and you fall to your knees,
still, gazing on the numberless roses,
silent, a garden spread just for this rest.

Julia, your shirt

is black and smells of wonderful stuff, flowers and herbs
crushed together in a marble mortar
imagine your face swathed with cobalt blue
like a lapis bust of Nefertiti pouting down the Nile
pull your chin up a little that's *perfect*

you say your shirt isn't really you it was a gift
you wouldn't have bought it because it has sort of pseudo art on it
but there's more than eyes at work here
there's the glorious smell of it, the fact that you were in it
your very own self while you went about your day
whatever it is it's the smell of you and your day
the aura of everything everyone that touched
julia
your shirt
every time I pass it I have to pick it up and smell it
won't you please come get it
help me get this shirt-scent out of my head
help me lead some kind of ordinary life

Praise Song

Oh, that he who poured the sea,
    flowing from his fingers
    arc gleam, falling
    should be enthroned upon my praise!

Oh, that he who scattered islands
    joyously, by handfuls,
    seeing their silver splash,
    should want me for his intimate!

Oh, that the splitter of the light
    to greater and to lesser,
    sunbright, moonflood,
    should ask to hear my deepest thoughts!

Oh, that the molder of the man,
    who like a wind gives life,
    dustchange, love breath,
    should crave my constant company!

God's hair

Can you remember God's hair?
Adam did
in evening cool.
Long, behind his ears.
But Adam
forgot.

Can you remember God's hair?
Around the head of Jacob
in flight,
locks pulled, flung,
wrestling
in the thick of arms
all the night.

Can you remember God's hair?
Darker moist,
matted
over thorn,
splinters
in it, pieces
of the scourge.
Black
like wet spikes
on his brow,
still
as carved,
crusted
with blood.

Can you remember God's hair?
  Tingling
    at cold air
      from door crack of the tomb.
        Blowing
          straight up
            at exit
              into light.

In Jerusalem God is a Chinese Waiter

letters like snow, like angels' dandruff, drift
into Jerusalem, letters to God

the postmaster tries to send them someplace
Hebrew ones to the Wailing Wall
Christian ones to Bethlehem
letters in Chinese are translated
once a week by the waiter

the unhinged write to God
retards, crazies, children, the senile
cast their bread on Jerusalem's waters

do they write send money
           wish You were here
           so long since I heard from You
           why haven't You returned my calls
           where the hell are You anyway?

or do they send blank pages
that say here I am, fill me up
and enclose a self-addressed stamped envelope?

Late Supper

Legs moonlit on the wind-cold sheets
Mattress on the floor
Dark bread
Dried fruit
Breasts like empty wineskins

God on his haunches

such an appalling picture
God on his haunches
like a bird watcher, waiting
for what he knows must happen
but will for the world neither impede nor hurry on
waiting for the crunch of the beak through the egg
waiting for the infusion of blue through the bud
God the time-lapse photographer

such a terrifying picture
that the Timeless One should savour time
should know the necessity of every second
should want to plunge me
into the deeps of every moment
drown me in the glory of that which has been made
raise me, sodden, into uncreated light
gleaming in the sun like a dolphin's back

a barbed baptism, the eternal end
reached only through fiery lungfuls of time
every second clotting the nostrils
each moment a coal ablaze in the throat